Love
ISN'T CONSTANT
PAIN
2

K. Rashad

Pink Butterfly Press
Publishing for the next generation

I would like to dedicate
this book to Daniel Caldwell.
Thank you for being there for me
during some of the darkest days of my life.
Thank you for believing in me.
Thank you for being a good friend,
teacher and mentor. Rest In Peace

Daddy's Little Girl

I think about all the hearts
I broke before you.
Now, it's my job to protect yours.
My baby girl, my world,
I want you to know that
I adore you.
That's why there are
a few things I have to teach you.
Like how to be a strong woman, always love yourself,
 and put yourself first, work hard and be independent
because most men aren't s***; trust me, I know.
You may not understand right now,
but you will as you grow.
"Daddy's Little Girl," I want you to know
that I would never neglect you;
make these men respect you;
I may not always be there to protect you!
I'm just letting you know.

You Can Do Better Than Me

It's funny how you keep finding your way back to me.
It confuses me because I know you can do much better
 than me. Some nights, I sit up, staring at you
 while you're sleeping, and ask myself,
What is it about me that you love so much?
What keeps you here? What keeps you coming back?
I don't ever think it's because you love me.
But if that's your reason,
then why do you love me? How could you love me?
For so long, I've done you so wrong,
caused you so much pain.
But even after all the hell I put you through,
 you remain loyal to me; you stay right by my side;
I don't understand it.
You're such a strong, good woman,
and I honestly don't deserve
 to be your man. When will you
 see and accept that truth?

Triggered

If you read something and it triggers you,
That means you still have a lot of healing to do.
You have to know your triggers to receive healing.

What Did You Learn?

Some people get so caught up in relationships
and love that they miss the lessons that heartbreak
might be trying to teach them.
We all need to learn these lessons
because we keep repeating toxic cycles.
Stop asking why they hurt you and start
asking what have they taught you?
Some experiences are worth
much more than your "feelings."

The Strongest Woman I Know

The strongest woman is the one who stopped running.
She's the one who isn't a prisoner to her fears.
She's the one who isn't a slave to her pain.
She's the one who isn't living in the past.
The strongest woman is the one who has
found peace despite all she's faced.

The Mask Falls Off

Only if you knew how much pain was hiding
behind this fake smile of mine.
For so many years, I've hidden my emotions behind this mask.
I pretended to be happy.
I acted like we were the perfect family.
I was too afraid to accept. "Accept what?" You may ask.
Accept the truth.
The truth is, I've been unhappy for a very long time.
Maybe I was holding on to what was.
I hoped that things would go back to the way things were.
"Hope." Yeah, that's what it was.
However, that same hope put me through so much pain.
Yet, I loved you. I was afraid to leave you
because I didn't want to hurt you,
but that never stopped you from hurting me.
I can no longer live like this anymore,
I'm sorry, but I can't do it anymore!
I can no longer pretend. I'm taking this mask off
and calling it quits; this is the end.
Although not the end for me, it's the end for us.

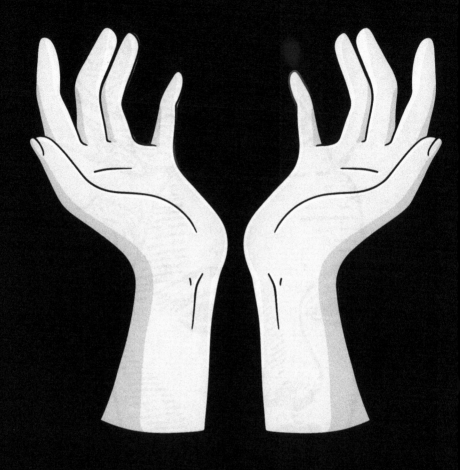

Lost Her

He didn't even realize that he was losing her,
but I could tell by the look in her eyes
that he had already lost her.

Never Learn

I wish I had known you before falling in love with you.
They say that what you ignore in the beginning,
you'll pay for in the end.
That's the price we all pay when we ignore all the signs.
We are left with nothing but pain and a lot of regrets.
We are left wishing we would've opened our eyes
and learned the lesson much sooner.
We can't always feel the ending. Sometimes we don't know when
it's going to come. Red flags? We look past them
because of our love for that special someone.
But those red flags we choose to look past will hurt us.
"How could I have been so stupid?"
We say. We begin sabotaging ourselves.
We select different people in the same circumstances,
make the same mistakes, and reap the same outcome.
Another failed relationship,
another heartbreak, another lesson.
A lesson that, sadly, most of us will never learn.

It's Time To Pour Into Yourself

You're tired and exhausted because
you have nothing left to give.
That's what happens when you spend most
of your time and energy pouring love
into people more than you do yourself.

That's Love

Many people are afraid to love,
but we shouldn't fear love because love
isn't the problem. It is our expectations
of others that cause us to love them.
That's the problem. You see, that's where
we all go wrong; that's where we mess up.
We believe that the harder we love someone,
and the more love we show them,
 the more they will love and appreciate us.
But you can't force love, and you can't persuade
someone into loving you. It doesn't matter how hard
you fight for them to see it because love can only be felt,
not seen. Love isn't perfect, but it's not about "perfect love."
It's about healthy love. It's about finding someone who shares
the same beliefs as you, someone who knows not only how to
receive love but also give love. True love will set your soul on
fire; once that fire ignites, it'll never stop burning.
A small flame could turn into a wildfire real quick.
We will grow together, we will learn, and we will burn.
And set the whole world on fire; that's love!

The Real Battle

*Separating how you feel from what you
actually "know" is the real battle.*

I Tried My Best

I've tried being patient,
but I don't know how to get through to you.
I have to go through a maze to get to you.
Every day I feel like I'm dealing with a different you.
Some nights I think about all the s*** you put me through.
Lost and confused, but I knew what I should do.
My heart feels for you, but my mind is so sick of you.
It's a constant battle, a battle I'm tired of; I don't know which
one to listen to. People say I should listen to my intuition.
But that's easier said than done; I'm stuck in a challenging
position. It will be one of my most complex decisions,
the hardest one for me to make.
Because I don't want to leave you, maybe we need a break.
Maybe we both need some time apart.
Before what we "have" turns into what we "had,"
I refuse to let our relationship fall apart.
Who am I kidding? It already did.
That's my pride and ego talking, and me just hiding behind
fear. I guess the only thing left for me to do, is to accept.
Know that I did love you, and I tried my best.

Fear Or Ego?

Sometimes, I wonder what happened between us.
Were you afraid, or was it just your big ego?
What made you push me away? What made you run away?
For whatever reason it was, I wish you would've fought harder.
Harder for me, harder for how you feel/felt, harder for us!

Sweet Memories

What do you do when your lover has changed,
but you're still in love with who they used to be?
Deep down inside, you know you don't love them anymore,
you're just still in love with the sweet memories.
Nothing's the same; although we know that,
it's still hard to accept. We try so hard to ignite that old flame.
Only to find out that that old flame doesn't burn the same.
"Here comes the pain."
Reminiscing about the first time y'all met.
Things were so perfect in the beginning.
Both can't get enough of each other,
and can't stop thinking of each other.
Making love three, or four times
a day. Suddenly all that begins
to fade away. People change,
and we only remain in love
with how things used to be.
You don't love them anymore,
you're just still in love with
the sweet memories.

No Do-Overs

It was never supposed to end
this way, "together forever,"
that's what we used to say.
I promised you a life full of love
and happiness, but I gave you nothing but years of betrayal and
heartbreak. Not many men can admit when they've lost a good
thing. I'd do anything to start over and take back all the
mistakes I've made, But life doesn't work that way,
and there are no do-overs. When I first met you,
I was willing to do whatever to win you.
Then, I got a little too comfortable once I got you.
I lost sight, the sight of you, the sight of us somehow,
our love ended up in the backseat.
I drifted off, and you were already distancing yourself
by the time I realized it. That's when reality began to
set in because I felt you slipping away.
I'd do anything to go back and fix where I went wrong,
But life doesn't work like that; there are no do-overs.

Too Late

When you start taking her seriously, it'll be too late.

Effort

What has he sacrificed for you?
What has he changed for you?
If your answer is nothing, then he doesn't love you.
Because love requires sacrifice, love requires change,
and love involves effort!

The Wrong Person

You shouldn't have to beg for love, loyalty, and respect.
You're asking for the right things,
just from the wrong person.

Trauma Bond

But, you see, we're both to blame for this pain.
I, first, for not knowing what love is or how to love.
Then you, for lack of self-love
and loving me more than you love yourself.

Forgive Yourself

"Do you have any regrets?"
"No, I don't," she says.
But do not judge me by my past
because I'm only human.
I don't mind talking about the mistakes I've made,
but I need you to understand, that I don't live
there anymore. I am not the woman I once was.
Yes, there are a lot of things I could've done
better. Like, loved me better, but the
first time I fell in love,
 I was so young and didn't know
any better.
Foolish girl, I was, lol.
I used to say to myself
that would never be me.
Now that we are talking about
it, I'm like,
"Nah, that couldn't
have been me."

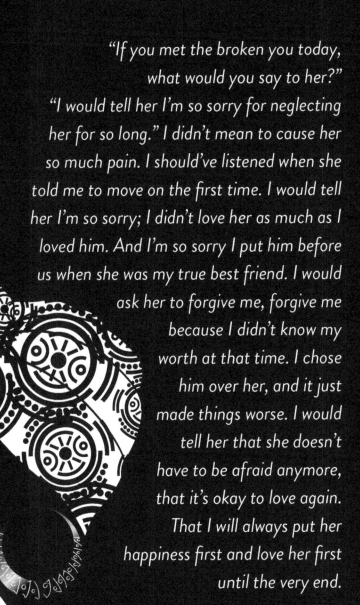

"If you met the broken you today,
what would you say to her?"
"I would tell her I'm so sorry for neglecting
her for so long." I didn't mean to cause her
so much pain. I should've listened when she
told me to move on the first time. I would tell
her I'm so sorry; I didn't love her as much as I
loved him. And I'm so sorry I put him before
us when she was my true best friend. I would
ask her to forgive me, forgive me
because I didn't know my
worth at that time. I chose
him over her, and it just
made things worse. I would
tell her that she doesn't
have to be afraid anymore,
that it's okay to love again.
That I will always put her
happiness first and love her first
until the very end.

The Journey

She's not yet the woman she knows she can be,
but she's learning.
Healing takes time, be patient with yourself.
Self-love is one long, hard, beautiful, endless journey.

Within

You come to me as if I have the power to set you free,
but you're turning to and relying on the wrong person.
The only way to become free is by looking within.
I know you're in pain and yearning to be loved,
but first, you must heal what's within.
Avoiding the process because you think it's too hard,
or because you think you're not strong enough,
will only invite more pain into your life.
Don't you think it's about time you did things right?
For many years, you've searched for love in others but never
yourself. The love your heart is yearning for is much
closer than you think. The happiness you're seeking
is much closer than you think. The freedom your soul
is craving for is much closer than you think. Go Within.

Band-Aid

We think people can love away all of our trauma and pain,
but it doesn't work that way.
We can't go through life using people as band-aids to
cover up our scars and wounds. There's no healing in that
because as soon as that band-aid falls off,
our wounds get exposed, and the pain creeps right back in.
Afraid or just not ready to deal with the pain, what do we do?
We panic and search for another band-aid,
hoping the next one will stay a little longer than the last one.

Coping

I enjoyed your company.
I appreciate everything you've done for me.
But I just don't feel the same.
I was just using you to cope because I was in pain. I'm sorry.
People will use you, then run back to the person who hurt them.

Unhealthy Attachment

There's no love, just a few good memories,
and an unhealthy attachment.

Completely Yours

She may give you her time,
but until she finds the strength to walk away from him
altogether, he will always have her heart and her mind.
Pursue her if you will, but I'm telling you now,
you're only going to end up hurt.
Mentally and emotionally, he still has a hold on her,
and until she breaks the hold, he has on her,
she will never be entirely yours.

Inner Work

I've made plenty of mistakes when it comes
to love and relationships,
and some of those mistakes I've made numerous times.
I get attached and fall in love with broken people way too soon.
I'm sure many of you can relate to something I still struggle with.
See, for me, when I meet a person who's been through so much
heartbreak and trauma, I just want to love away all of their pain.
I just want to show them that not all people are the same,
but then I ask myself, are the people we love
or wish to be loved by the ones to blame?
Maybe, the problem isn't them.
Maybe, there's something about ourselves that we need
to change. People jump from relationship to relationship,
in search of someone to make their broken heart whole again.
As if it's their responsibility to fix them, but we are responsible
for our healing. A crucial lesson we all need to learn is that
we cannot love away someone's pain. And we cannot
build anything healthy or a solid foundation, by ignoring
a person's trauma, behavior, and toxic patterns.
We have to do inner work, or there will be no changes.
We will not find love; the only thing we will attract are trauma
bonds, unhealthy attachments, and false connections.

A Good Man

A good man will not come to you because you don't believe there's one. God will not bless you with something you don't believe in. Your belief that there are no good men and your lack of faith in love, is what's stopping you from experiencing something different, something healthy, something real, something new!

Love Is Unfamiliar

The more he hurts you doesn't
mean the more he loves you.
If you believe that you've been
wrong about what love is,
if all you know is pain, then you
genuinely don't know what
it's like to be loved by a man.
Now, I see why you don't believe in or have faith in love.
You've spent most of your life giving your love to all the
wrong men, but have never really been loved. You constantly put
your heart on the line, only to get broken every time. "Damn."
Just when you thought you'd found the right one
you find yourself drowning in a river of pain, hoping that
someday the right man will come and save you. Your sour
experiences have pushed you so far away from love, and your
pain you've become a slave to. Love is unfamiliar to you; pain is
what you're used to. It makes sense now; it does. You've never
been loved and don't know what love is. The pain he constantly
puts you through doesn't mean he loves you.

You Are The One To Blame

Many say, "the heart wants what it wants."
But if what it wants is doing nothing but hurting you,
and you continue to pursue it,
you can't blame anyone for your pain but yourself.

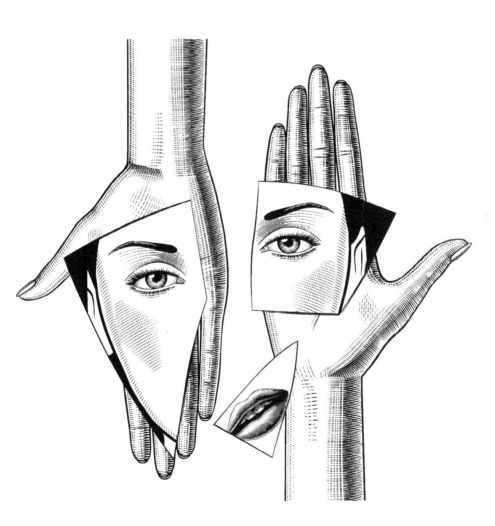

Misery Loves Company

You want everyone else to be unhappy because you're unhappy.
You once said to me, "you see beauty in nothing" well, maybe
that's why your life is so ugly. You believe in nothing;
you lack faith, no compassion, and most importantly,
you don't love yourself. You must heal and release the hate you
carry in your heart because your life becomes the energy you
walk in, but I understand you still have much healing to do.
I see why you're so angry, bitter, and miserable.
You haven't yet learned to let go.

Release

Your heart's filled with so much pain, anger,
and regrets, that love can't even get to you or get through you.
You've been holding on to past hurts for way too long.
It's time to let go!

What's Best For Her

She thought she was just being a good woman,
but now she sees where she went wrong.
She was so focused on making him happy,
that she lost sight of herself and forgot
about her needs and happiness.
It's always been that way for her.
She gets so deeply involved in her relationships
that she forgets about herself.
She's the kind of girl who loves hard
and wants what's best for her man,
but the sad thing is that no man has ever
matched her energy or wanted what's best for her.

All Of Her

She's not ashamed of her scars; she will not hide her pain.
She wants you to see her because she wants you to love her,
all of her! Her joy and her pain, the beauty and the ugly.

Scars

Why do you hide your scars?
Why are you so ashamed of them?
When I look at you, I see a unique piece of art.
To be honest with you, the ugly parts
of you I find the most beautiful.
They are the parts of you I'm most attracted to.
That's the side of you I would like to get to know.
The side of you nobody sees, the side of you,
you don't share with many people.
The side of you many men never took the time to understand.
"The Real You"
Because it is our scars and what we've
been through that make us who we are.
Every scar has its own story to tell.
I'm eager to know your story, and I want to hear every detail.
How can I love you without knowing your pain?
I want to know what made you the woman you are today.
Please share with me your mistakes, battles, pain, and suffering.
Share with me the lessons you've learned, your growth,
your journey and what inspired your change.
Please show me your scars; I want to see every one of them.
I want to feel everything you've been through.

Inner Strength

I wasn't searching for her pain;
I was searching for her inner strength,
Because even though she might not have known or believed it.
I knew she was much stronger than she thought.
There's a side of her she hasn't even met yet,
I just wanted to help her see it.
I just wanted to help bring that side out of her.

False Hope

False hope destroyed more women than love ever did.

Who They Are

They may never be who you want them to be.
They may never be who you need them to be.
All they can be is who they are, and if who they
currently are isn't enough for you, then, maybe it's
time for you to move on and find someone who is.
You cannot mold a person into the perfect lover,
no matter how much potential you may see in them.
No matter how hard you love them, no matter how hard you
fight for that person. You cannot change their ways.
Who they are is who they are. Yes, it's a hard pill to swallow,
but it's a truth we all must learn to accept.

Endings

When God brings death to a relationship,
no matter how much you try to make it work,
you can't bring it back to life.
You either learn to accept it and move on or die with it.

His Actions

"What are you looking for?"
"What do you want, and where do you see us going with this?"
Ask questions, but also pay attention to his actions.
Because it isn't just about what he's telling you;
what is he showing you?

Boundaries

*A man who doesn't respect your boundaries
will never respect you.*

It Wasn't For You

It fell apart because it wasn't for you.
It fell apart because you learned what you needed
to for that season. It fell apart because God has
something better waiting for you.

Homewrecker

I'm not trying to be a homewrecker,
but I can see you're not happy.
How does he call himself your man but doesn't value you,
and always makes you feel so small?
I hate seeing a good woman suffer.
It's hard not to get in between you both,
and I'm not trying to tell you what to do.
It's just crazy how he's been your man for so long,
and I care about your feelings more than he does.
I'm not trying to be a homewrecker;
that's not even my intention.
But how can I wreck a home that has fallen apart already?
How can I wreck a home that's been
falling apart for years now, brick by brick?
You may not want to hear what I'm saying, but I'm just
speaking the truth. He destroyed your home long ago;
if anything, he's the homewrecker!

Another Man

He holds onto her for the wrong reasons.
He doesn't want to let her go,
but he doesn't want to do what he needs to keep her.
As ironic as it sounds, it has nothing to do with love.
He doesn't want to see her happy with another man.
He'd rather she stays attached to him
and be miserable before setting her free.
In his delusional mind, he's the only man for her.

The Last Day

There's going to be a man who's going to be willing,
to do all the things you're not willing to do.
A man who is going to put her first, and she's going
to love every bit of it, because you always put her last.
He will remind her who she was before she met you
and help her find herself again.
He's going to put the brightest smile on her face.
When she finally meets this man,
I promise you that will be the last day
she will ever cry over you.

Karma

You've spent most of your life destroying
and toying with women.
I see love is just a game to you,
I see right through you; yeah,
I know your type, because I used to be just like you.
I could never promise a woman forever,
but we can chill for tonight.
Feeding them lies to get in between their thighs.
Playing with their feelings confuses them,
but you see that isn't right. Putting them through problems,
we wouldn't even put up with ourselves.
It's a different story when the shoes are on the other foot,
and our feelings are being hurt.
And we're the ones getting cheated on.
You felt that; that's anger you feel.
See, even the thought of her being with
another man triggers you.
I don't know why we think we're free to do whatever we want,
but it's a different story when they do us wrong.
Knowing we deserved every bit of it. "KARMA"

What If He Told You The Truth

What if he told you the truth?
What if he confessed that he's cheating on you?
Could you handle the raw truth?
Could you handle him looking you right in your eyes,
while he's telling you how he's torn in between the two?
That whenever he's with you, he's thinking of her?
Every time he comes home to you, he wishes it was her.
If he could, he would keep the both of you.
That he loves you, but he loves her too,
and the only reason why he keeps coming back home to you,
is because he loves you the most. He prefers the sex he has
with her, but he loves the security you give him and the
benefits of dating you. What if he told you the truth?
What if he told you that he's been sleeping with her for a few
months? And that he's been keeping this hidden from you,
but she knows all about you. Maybe that's the reason why he's
always trippin' on you, all this time, you thought he was just
insecure, but it's just guilt eating him alive. All this time,
he accused you of cheating and didn't like that you were
so friendly. When he's been the snake in disguise.
What if he told you the raw truth and not a lie?
What if he exposed his true self?
Could you handle it, or would you prefer he did not
and keep living a lie? What if?

Different Kinda Pain

*Falling for someone who will never be committed
to you is a different kind of pain.*

The Deep End

Why would you tell her to let her guard down, only to let her down? Why would you take her out to the deep end, only to watch her drown? If this is what you call love? She doesn't want it. If this is how you love her, she doesn't need it; you can keep it. She loved you unconditionally, accepted you for who you are, your flaws, and all. She loved you without judging, and even that was hard for her. She loved you, even when you no longer deserved her love. She loved you, even after all the times you did her wrong. She took you back with open arms. She loved you more than anyone has ever loved you. She cared more than anyone has ever cared for you. She forgave you, even when she was scared to because her intuition told her not to. She knew you would only hurt her again, but she ignored it because she was in love, and just wasn't ready to accept or believe it was the end. Why would you tell her to let her guard down, only to let her down? Why would you take her out to the deep end, only to watch her drown? Knowing damn well she loved you!

Just Like Him

How do you not respect women,
when your mother sacrificed so much for you?
When your father left, your mother took care of
the household and loved and protected you.
Does that mean nothing to you?
We both know your mother didn't raise you that way.
And don't say you're the way you are
because your father wasn't there.
Maybe, that is part of the problem, but it's still a sorry
excuse because my father wasn't there for me either.
Yes, we may share the same upbringing
and can relate to the same pain, but I'm nothing like you.
You were supposed to grow up and be a better man,
not just like him!

Genuine Heart

A genuine heart will never lose;
it only loses everyone who never deserved it.
And if you ask me, that isn't a loss at all.
It's a blessing,
because it makes room for someone who does.

Invisible

It's been five years, and he still doesn't see her.
After five years of her crying out for his love
and attention, he still doesn't hear her.
Throughout the years, she's grown so miserable.
It's like he doesn't even care,
and she's so damn tired of feeling invisible.

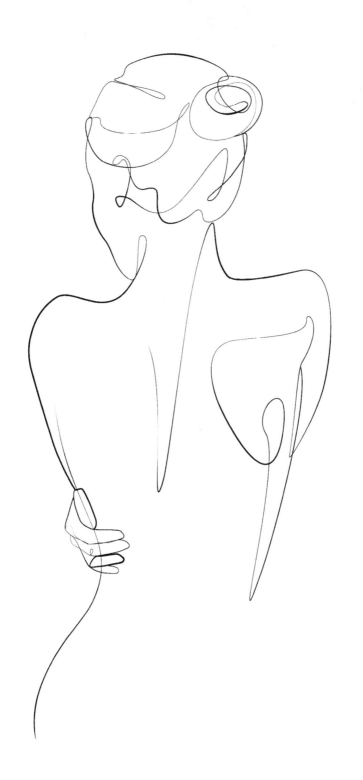

I See You, I Hear You, I Feel You

Troubled past,
I could only imagine the obstacles you had to go through.
I could only imagine the things you had to live through.
Still, I love you without judging you.
I wish I could've been there for you during those times,
but I understand you did what you had to do.
Don't ever feel ashamed of your past life.
We've all done things we aren't proud of; sadly, some
things we can't take back. All we can do is move forward;
moving backward, we can't afford to do.
No woman should go through what you've been through,
but you know what they say, our experiences make us who
we are, and who you were isn't the woman you are today.
You don't have to be perfect, and I don't care about the skeletons
in your closet. You don't have to hide the parts of yourself you're
insecure about. I still love and accept you fully because I see
beyond all your flaws.I see your strength. I see your potential.
I know who you are becoming. I see your growth.
I see your change. I see the light that shines brightly within you.
If only you could see yourself through my eyes.
You'd see the most beautiful woman you've ever seen.
You should start seeing yourself in that light too.

Picasso

If I could paint the perfect picture,
It would be a beautiful painting of you.
My Mona Lisa, My Juliet,
My Picasso piece would be you.

Don't You Ever

You've been through a lot,
and I understand how you feel.
I'm not judging you at all.
You have every reason to feel how you feel,
but I don't care how hurt or broken you feel.
Even if you temporarily give up on love,
don't you ever give up on yourself!

Stronger Than Ever

*She hasn't given up; she's just a bit tired
and needs some time to recover.
She'll learn to love again, and when that day comes,
her heart will be stronger than ever.*

The Cycle

It's not that I don't want to be with you,
but before I can love you,
you must first learn to love yourself.
I've watched you jump from relationship to relationship.
In and out of relationships with different partners but always
the same outcome. I'm just saying maybe you should
give relationships a break and focus on yourself,
because you'll be better off without a man right now.
Why is being alone so hard for you?
Why doesn't your happiness matter to you?
It's like you don't even care, as long as you have a body
next to you. The crazy thing is, that you don't even notice
the patterns. It just became so customary to you.
If I was to love you now, I feel like I'd be just another man passing
through. I'm telling you, we'll only crash because there's just
so much pain you haven't yet healed from your past.
You can't keep living this way. You can't keep loving this way.
So, for now, I think it's just best for me to stay away or for us to
just remain friends. It's not that I don't want to be with you.
I know I can love you correctly, but I also know I can't love away
your pain. Before we even think about love and being together,
heal first and make peace with your pain.
Right here, right now, is where this vicious cycle ends!

Enough Is Enough

Only a weak man wants to keep you confused and delusional.
Especially a narcissistic man.
He doesn't want you to be around anyone or listen to anything.
That might inspire you, empower you,
and give you the strength to say, Enough Is Enough!

Empowerment

Real love isn't toxic, controlling, or manipulative.
Real love is peace, freedom, and empowerment.
A real man doesn't take away your power, he empowers you!

Manipulation

Some people aren't really in love with you,
they are obsessed with the control they have over you.
For some, it's like a drug, and it feeds them.
The pushing and pulling, building and breaking you.
It's like they enjoy watching you lose your mind over them.
Dangerous people they are, especially when they know,
they got you right where they want you
"right in the palm of their hand."

Emotions

When you have no control over your emotions,
your emotions control your life,
and when your emotions control your life,
people will feed off and use those very same
emotions to control you.

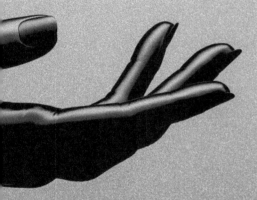

Disappointment

She's been through so much pain,
that's why she questions any man
who brings happiness into her life.
She immediately starts thinking the worst if it feels
too good to be true. But could you blame her?
She has a history full of men,
Who has done nothing but disappoint her.
Her past experiences make happiness so hard to embrace.

The Real You

You hide behind this wall you've built
and keep all of your emotions bottled up.
You don't even express yourself.
How can anyone learn to love the "real you."
when you're so afraid to show them the real you?

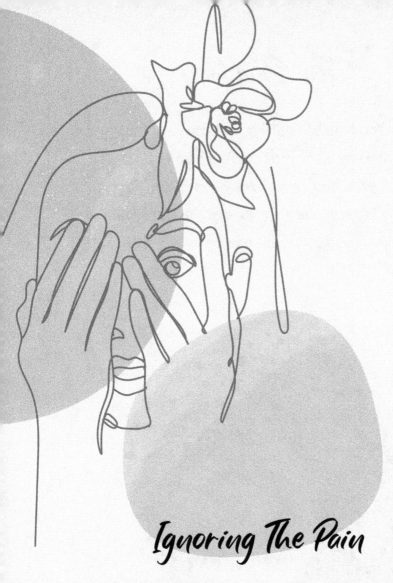

Ignoring The Pain

You want to know why it's taking you so long to heal, because instead of you being honest with yourself and your emotions, you pretend everything's perfect and you're not hurt. But you are.

Clarity

Healing starts with acceptance,
and acceptance will give you freedom.
You're not always going to get clarity.
Sometimes, we must trust that whatever
happens is happening for a reason.
Because there are some things, you're not going
to understand until later on. There are some questions
you may never get the answers to.

Big Mistake

Staying too long was her mistake.
But losing her was yours!

Once You Heal

And once you heal, he's not going to like the new you.
He's going to hate your strength.
He's going to hate your confidence.
He's going to hate how much you've grown to love yourself.

Butterfly

She was the butterfly nobody could catch,
and I was the flower in the garden she hadn't landed on just yet.
Waiting patiently, hoping someday, she will.

Take Your Time

We barely even know each other,
and we're talking about how much we love each other.
I would say that's where a lot of us go wrong.
We fall in love with people before we get to know them.
It's all so cute in the beginning, until time goes by,
and slowly, they reveal their true colors.
Then you start seeing how ugly they are.
Usually, by that time, it's a little too late,
and then we wish we would've taken our time.

Back Door

I've been knocking on this door for some time now;
maybe I should try the doorbell. Damn, the doorbell's broken.
I can see someone peeking from behind the curtain.
It's her; I know it's her. There she goes hiding as always.
Are you going to let me in? "No!" she yells. "Never!"
She had a sign on her heart that said,
"Keep out, no men allowed." (Private property)
this isn't my first rodeo with her. Cool, I'll be back,
but I'm not knocking next time. I'm kicking the door down!
At the time, that's how I felt, but I would never do that.
The last man she let in had already caused enough damage.
Tonight, I'll rest and try another day.
"Rest" is something I didn't get. I spent most of the night
thinking. There has to be a key; if I could find that key,
she might let me in. I couldn't give up. Now, here I am, right back
at her front door again, but before I could knock, a man opened
the door and asked, "Who are you?" Damn, how did he get in?
I thought to myself. Here I am trying to be a gentleman and do
things the right way, and this man snuck in through the back
door. "I'm nobody," I replied. "I was just in the neighborhood
checking out the property. What a beautiful home you have."
A few weeks later, I saw a 'for rent sign on the door, but I wasn't
surprised. The tenants never stay too long.

Looks Are Deceiving

They fall in love with their eyes, not with their hearts.
What looks good to the eyes isn't always good for your heart.

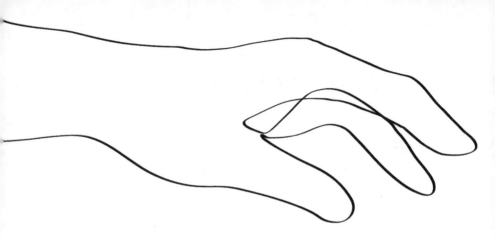

Safe

I hold her tightly as if she was my child who ran into my arms,
frightened. By the cracking sounds of the thunderstorm.
With the soothing sound of the raindrops,
the sky darkens from the clouds.
The whistling wind blows, and the night owl hoots.
It's been a while since I've shared a bed with someone.
I got so used to sleeping alone.
Goodnight, my love; gently, I give her a forehead kiss.
I gently run my fingers through her hair,
holding her with the other hand.
She sleeps peacefully with no worries at all.
My love is her cover, and my chest is her pillow.
In my arms, she always feels safe.

Loved Correctly

Some would say that she's spoiled.
But I wouldn't call it "spoiled," she's just loved correctly.

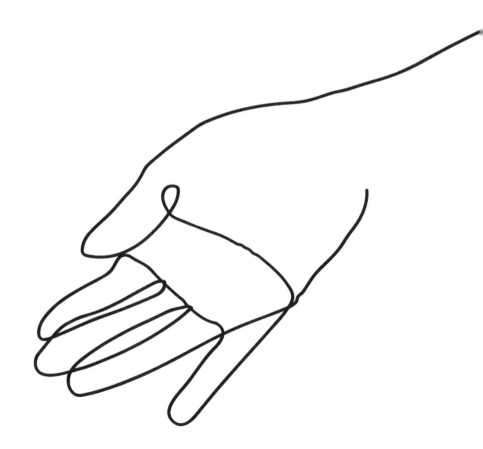

Wounded Warrior

*Heart full of battle scars, we shared the same pain,
and our stories were very similar. Our bodies were covered
with knife scars and bullet wounds from past battles.
We've both fought in the same war, narcs vs. empaths.
People who feel so much against people who have no
emotions at all. I know exactly how it feels to go to war for
someone who wouldn't even fight for you. Ready and willing to
sacrifice all that you have and everything that you are.
Knowing damn well they wouldn't do the same for you,
But I guess that's what warriors do. We shared a special
connection because I'm a wounded warrior too.
I can relate to the betrayals, heartbreaks,
and wars she's been through.*

Hurt The Most

If I ever needed her, no matter the time of day,
she was there for me right away.
There's nothing like having someone in your life who truly cares.
I never once questioned her loyalty or if she loved me.
There's nothing more valuable than
a strong, loving, and loyal woman.
Sadly, so many of them are overlooked and unappreciated,
and they are usually the ones who get hurt the most.

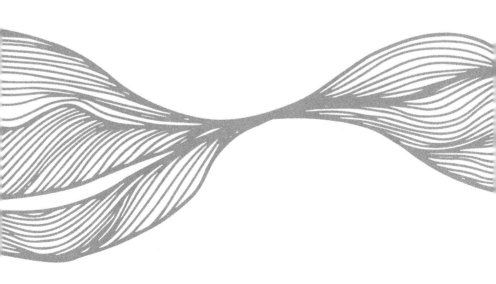

Without Judging Them

I always give her some of the best advice;
that's why she loves talking to me.
A woman wants a man who listens to her and understands her.
She wasn't used to opening up; she kept her emotions bottled up.
She was the "it is what it is, kinda girl,"
but she expressed herself well with me.
She tells me everything; we would talk on the phone for hours,
because she's comfortable and she trusts me.
I listen without judging her.
I just give her advice; I don't tell her how
to live or judge her by her mistakes.
I understand she has to live with her decisions, not me.
I've learned that women don't want to be treated
or yelled at like they're little girls.
They don't want to be told what they should or shouldn't do.
Sometimes, they just want you to listen.
Sometimes, they just want to be able to express themselves
and get honest feedback. Without you judging them.

She Chose You

Out of every man she could've been with, she chose you.
Even after she promised herself,
she would never get involved in another relationship again.
Even when she decided she was just going to focus on herself,
she didn't want a friend.
But then you came along, and she let you in.
She decided to give you a chance and another shot at love.
Even with all the fear and anxiety, she had to overcome.
Even with her overthinking and the nightmares she had
of being hurt again. Out of every man she
could've been with, she chose you.
She regrets everything she ever told you,
because you did nothing but take advantage of her.
You knew how vulnerable she was.
You knew her heart couldn't take any more scars.
Initially, you should've told her you weren't looking for love.
She trusted you and stepped out of her comfort zone.
She gave you a chance.
A chance so many men before you would've loved to have.
Out of every man she could've been with, she chose you.

Relationship Goals

He's no good for her, and she knows it too, but for some
strange reason, she still loves him. For some strange reason,
she doesn't want to let him go. Too complicated to explain,
but I understand her love for him and can relate to her pain.
It's like being under a love spell, a love spell that is so hard to
break. They look so in love, don't they? Little do they know
that smile she walks around with is fake. "Relationship goals.
I wish I had a man who loved me the way your man loves you,"
her friend says. Silly girl, her friend doesn't have a clue.
She has no idea how many nights she stayed up crying.
If she could, she would trade places with you.
Life is already a battle. She hates getting off from work
only to go home and fight another war. They look so in love,
don't they? But nobody sees what goes on behind closed doors.
What's the point in looking good together, if we don't feel good
together? You'd be surprised how many people post pictures,
pretending like they're a happy family. Daddy's never home,
Mommy's always at work, and no one pays attention to the child.
"Relationship goals." Many live their lives through social media,
but nobody knows what goes on in their relationships behind
closed doors. So think twice before yelling "relationship goals."

Dancing In The Rain

She wasn't the young lady I had met in the past.
It's been such a long time since I last saw her.
So much about her has changed.
Her energy and confidence were so much different than before.
We talked about life and her self-love journey,
and I must say I was amazed at how much
she's grown mentally and emotionally.
She knows what she wants,
and this time, she refuses to settle for less.
She knows her worth now and has grown to love herself.
Yes, she made lots of mistakes, but she learned,
And she promised herself,
that she would never make those mistakes again.
She puts herself; first; she's so much stronger.
She survived the worst. She walks with a different energy,
and her aura has changed.
No longer living a life full of heartbreak and pain,
she's more balanced, more peaceful.
She used to run from the storm
but now enjoys dancing in the rain.

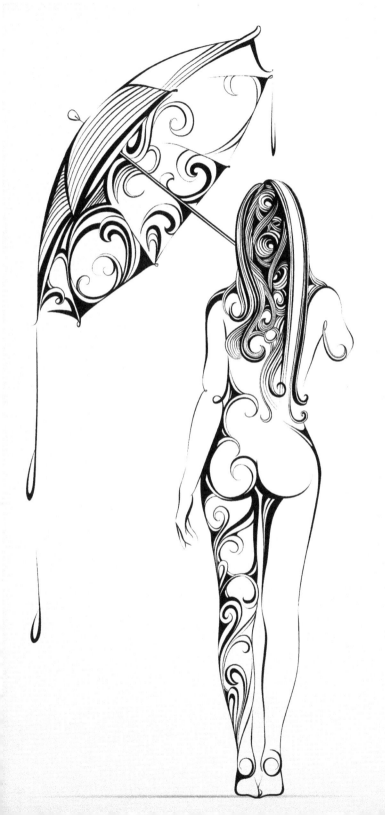

Urban Legend

No regrets, no looking back.
Hurt but not broken.
I was asleep, but now I'm woken.
Confident and outspoken.
Let me tell you a story about a little boy who became a man,
and a man who became a beast.
Misunderstood, overlooked, and slept on.
Humble but never weak.
Outstanding strength, fearless, and passionate
A great fire burns deep beneath (Phoenix).
Lost count of how many times he died and rise (Transformation).
Storms, he's not afraid of them.
Battles, he's used to them.
Those who doubted him, he laughs at them (Fools).
They underestimated his strength.
His mind's as sharp as any dagger or knife.
He has the heart of a lion, a warrior's soul.
When he dies, stories will be told!

Be Proud

It feels good, doesn't it?
The peace, the freedom, to finally be happy
and be no longer at war with yourself.
I'm so proud and happy that you're learning to love yourself,
and you should be too!

Thank You

To all the people who hurt me, I don't hate y'all.
I love all of you, and I want to thank y'all,
Because of y'all, I've learned to love myself first.
Because of y'all, I now see and know my worth.

My Mother's Child

I am my mother's child.
I feel and carry my mother's pain.

Affirmations

I Am Strong
I Am Beautiful I Am Worthy
I Am More Than Enough

CPSIA information can be obtained
at www.ICGtesting.com
Printed in the USA
LVHW011546301122
733863LV00018B/990/J

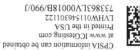